THE MOLL GUNSMITHS

By Earl S. Heffner, Jr.

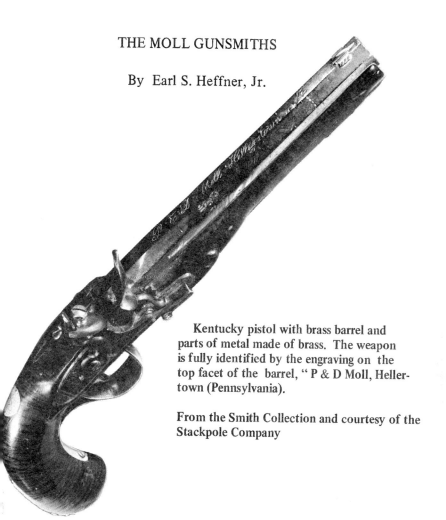

Kentucky pistol with brass barrel and parts of metal made of brass. The weapon is fully identified by the engraving on the top facet of the barrel, " P & D Moll, Hellertown (Pennsylvania).

From the Smith Collection and courtesy of the Stackpole Company

Published especially for the Hellertown, Northampton County Centennial Celebration.

The School of the Ozarks
Book Division
1972

Offset and Bound in the United States of America at
The School of the Ozarks, Point Lookout, Missouri 65726

Acknowledgments—

The author gratefully acknowledges the help and cooperation of Henry J. Kauffman, Ed Minner, Paul Beret, Henry Nonnemaker, Robert Limons, and Isabel Y. Bauder in the preparation of this manuscript.

DEDICATION

This book is dedicated to Victor L. Johnson and John J. Reed of the Department of History of Muhlenberg College, Allentown, Pennsylvania, whose influence on my life has been immeasurable.

TABLE OF CONTENTS

THE MOLL GUNSMITHS

I. INTRODUCTION

This paper is an attempt to record and interpret some of the activities of six generations of local gunsmiths. The work is in no way complete or definitive, nor does the author pretend it to be so. However, every effort was made to insure a collection of facts that would tend to reduce the obscurity of the gunsmiths in question. It is my purpose to present the facts concerning the Molls in an easily comprehensible form, to enlighten local inhabitants as to the proper place the Molls should have in history, to correct glaring errors of facts and unqualified misrepresentations, legends, and local hearsay, and to promote and stimulate an interest in local history by probing into the past for the truth and evaluating it on the basis of the events that took place.

The subjects of this paper, William, John I, John II, John III, James, William H., Peter, David, Nathan, and John J. Moll, were fine Pennsylvania gunsmiths. Their activities spanned five critical periods of American history in which their products were a major factor in the determination of the success of our country. These periods were the settlement of the Colonies—when the rifle was the primary tool of the pioneer in the wilderness, the Revolutionary War—when Yankee riflemen played havoc on the British forces with expert marksmanship at long ranges, The War of 1812—when the rifle protruding from bales of cotton at New Orleans provided us with the only significant land victory of the war, the Civil War—when the rifle produced in the industrial North helped to preserve the Union, the settlement of the West—when the rifle repulsed the Indian, killed off the buffalo, and settled many differences outside of court.

It is difficult to fully understand and appreciate the hardship, poverty, and bitter reverses that faced the early pioneers in America. The frontier life in Pennsylvania in general and Allentown in particular was hard and uncertain. The Walking Purchase, the French and Indian War, squatters exerting their rights, robbing and general abuse of the Indian, among other things, contributed to form a highly combustible situation in the area that is now Lehigh County. The Indian Councils in Easton in the years 1756, 1757, 1758, 1759, and 1761 somewhat relieved the tension. Yet, even as late as October 1763 the settlers around Allentown were subject to Indian raids. A letter from Colonel James Burd to William Allen dated January 10, 1764 states, "On the Saturday morning the town of Northampton was crowded with men, women, and children, flying from the enemy whom they said was within a few miles of the town killing all before them and burning the houses, upon which I collected the men of the town together in order to make a stand and save the people, with the place; but found only four Guns in the town, one of which my own and two out of order and no ammunition."[1] The settlers, exposed to the enemy and attacks of animals, murder by the Indians, and property destruction, needed an element of stability injected into their society—they needed a gunsmith. The Molls effected the stability of the community by producing weapons that could deal with the threats to their security.

The Molls were manufacturers of the Pennsylvania Rifle or Kentucky Rifle, if you prefer. The name Kentucky Rifle was adopted by the layman because of the popularization it

2

had received in the hands of Daniel Boone. Actually the home of the Pennsylvania Rifle was in Lancaster County where ample natural resources provided the best environment for its production. It was in Lancaster that most apprenticeships were served, and it was from Lancaster that the migration of gunsmiths to other colonies and counties, such as Lehigh and Northampton, took place. The average Pennsylvania Rifle weighed approximately seven to ten pounds, had an overall length varying between fifty-five and sixty inches of which the barrel length comprised forty to forty-four inches. The caliber was approximately forty-five (.45). The cost of the gun was directly related to the amount of gold, silver, brass, and bone inlays that adorned it. Thus, because of individual tastes, the cost of the rifle could vary from ten to fifty dollars. The barrels were hand-forged in charcoal fires and were bored by primitive tools. Everything was handmade and the process was slow and tedious. The rifles were accurate to about three hundred yards, depending upon the number of riflings in the barrel. The average Pennsylvania Rifle had either five or seven riflings. The Pennsylvania Rifle was truly an American product designed and produced to meet a pressing need. That we enjoy the type of government that we do today is, in large part, due to these insignificant German and Swiss craftsmen. The Pennsylvania Rifle was the indispensable tool of the pioneer. It provided him with protection against the Indian, provided him with a full larder of game, aided him in his struggle for freedom, fulfilled a part of his recreation, and gave him somewhat of a sense of security.

FOOTNOTES I

1. Roberts, Charles R., et al., **History of Lehigh County, Pennsylvania**, Vol. I, p. 393.

II. THE EARLY MOLLS AND THE REVOLUTION

The first Moll gunsmith with whom we come in contact is a certain William Moll. The only concrete information that could be obtained about him is the fact that he left a riflemaking tool to his heirs. The tool contained the inscription "April 10, 1747—W.M." His great-grandson, William H. Moll, is supposed to have had the tool in his possession.[2] Inquiries concerning the location of the tool have proved negative. I doubt whether William Moll lived in the Allentown area as some would have us believe. There is no record of William Moll on Northampton County tax lists; nor does his name appear on any ship's list in the Port of Philadelphia; nor is there any record of indenture for him. Evidently he was dead by the time of the Revolutionary War, since his name does not appear among those who took the oath of allegiance nor among those who refused to take it. Also, there is no record of his ownership of property in this area. This William Moll was the father of John Moll whom I shall henceforth call John Moll I for the purpose of clarification.

The first record that we have of John Moll I is on the Northampton tax list for the year 1764, the same year that the Paxton Boys marched to Philadelphia to demand reforms.[3] This tax list for the year 1764 included twenty-eight taxables. This was an increase of 12 persons from the

5

year 1763. He was taxed 6 pounds. Strangely enough, in 1765 the names on this year's tax list coincided with those of the list of the previous year with the notable exception of John Moll. The reason for this deletion remains unexplained.

The community was growing. Numerous tradesmen, such as potters, tailors, blacksmiths, masons, shoemakers, joiners, and bakers appeared in the community as the number of houses jumped from thirty-five in 1766 to forty-three in 1768.[4]

In 1772 John Moll I married Lydia Rinker. The ceremony was performed by the Reverend Mr. Abraham Blumer of the Zion Reformed Church, Allentown, on April 28, 1772.[5] Evidently they resided in Allentown, for John Moll I is listed as a resident of the town in Matthew S. Henry's *Manuscript History of Northampton County* as "John Moll, Gunsmith".[6]

Some writers would have us believe that John Moll I was an innkeeper before he became a gunsmith. However, I have found cause to dispute this theory in that John Moll I is always listed as a gunsmith on the tax lists. In the case of a dual occupation both are listed on the tax records. This was not the case with John Moll I. It is true that the Lafayette Hotel which was destroyed by fire in 1927 did have its origin in the Black Horse Tavern which was erected by Mr. Moll. However, the hotel was not erected until 1812 and the first proprietor was a Mr. Daniel Moyer.[7] I am convinced that John Moll I was engaged as a gunsmith years before the Revolutionary War, therefore I do not agree with the theory that he was ever engaged in innkeeping.[8]

The first record of a purchase of property by John Moll I is a deed dated March 19, 1773. The transaction took place with Melchior Tanner. The two agreed that for the sum of forty-five pounds John Moll was to receive a lot or piece of ground "containing in breth on Allens Street (now North Seventh Street) Sixty feet and debth two hundred and thirty feet in Northampton Town. To hold to him the said John

Moll and his Heirs and his Assigns forever under the yearly ground rent of Nine Shillings Sterling Money of Great Britain to the Chiefe Lord or Lords of the Fee thereof."[9] This property was to remain in the family for more than a hundred years.

While antagonism with the mother country was growing stronger each day, John Moll settled with his new bride in the peaceful village of Allentown. He was probably unaware of the great conflict to come. On May 13, 1773, seven months before the Boston Tea Party, a son John, whom I shall henceforth call John Moll II for the purpose of clarification, was born.[10] The First and Second Continental Congresses had met and Bunker Hill was history when in March of 1776, a second son, John J., was born to the Molls.[11] A third son, Peter, was born November 26, 1779.[12]

Northampton County, in the abovementioned period, again had its domestic tranquillity disturbed. Patriots pressured Tories out of the county. Plans were made for the raising of a militia and an election was held to select men for the Committee of Safety in the county. The burden of supplying a military force logistically fell heavily upon the fertile countryside. Requisitions for food, grain, cattle, horses and cloth became commonplace to the inhabitants. Northampton County not only gave freely of supplies, but also of manpower in both the military and industrial fields. There was quite some excitement when Danny Morgan came to Bethlehem and established his headquarters there in the hope of getting recruits. He was quite successful; in fact, three hundred men volunteered for his forces. Men were chosen on the basis of marksmanship. It is said "that the enlisting officer drew a man's nose on a blackboard and announced that only those men closest to the mark would be accepted. It was a severe test for the distance was great but everyone who took the test hit the nose."[13] This is a lovely picture, all the young men rushing toward the recruiting officers with their deadly accurate Pennsylvania Rifles in hand hoping that they would hit the nose on the blackboard and all did, but highly unrealistic and exaggerated. There were undoubtedly eager, adventurous young men who flocked to the call of arms, but knowing something of the provinciality of the Germans of Pennsylvania, I would be inclined to believe that most were reluctant to go marching to Boston, of all places, with Morgan, even though the conflict was still relatively young.

I have mentioned previously that men of the county also aided in the production of military goods. Early in the conflict gunsmithing was placed in the virtual control of the Continental Congress which fixed the prices of the guns and also decreed that all guns should be delivered to the patriot army upon pain of the gunsmiths being branded as enemies and of being deprived of the tools of their trade if they refused. Pennsylvania riflemakers helped greatly to supply the nine companies of militiamen that were raised in the state.[14] Northampton County exempted all of her gunsmiths from military service provided that they engaged in their trade during the war.[15] Some of the gunsmiths, however, volunteered and served admirably with the troops as artificers and repairmen.

At the outbreak of the Revolution, Allentown had only three hundred and fifty inhabitants. The majority of these people conformed to the Act of the Assembly of Pennsylvania which prescribed for Oaths of Affirmation and Allegiance. On June 8, 1778, John Moll I swore to the following:

> I do swear and affirm that I will renounce and refuse all allegiance to George the Third, King of Great Britain, his heirs and successors; and that I will be faithful and bear true allegiance to the Commonwealth of Pennsylvania. as a free and independent state, and that I will not at any time do or cause to be done any matter or thing that

will be prejudicial or injurious to the freedom and independence thereof as declared by Congress: and also that I will discover and make known to some one Justice of the Peace of said State all treason or traitorous conspiracies which I now know or hereafter shall know to be formed against this or any of the United States of America.[16]

To appreciate the feelings or thoughts that were in John Moll's mind when he took the oath is impossible. If he had reservations, and I doubt that he had many, the social ostracism, the deprival of tools, and the difficulty of providing for a family may have entered his mind along with the concept of freedom and liberty that he expected to enjoy in the case of victory. John Moll I took the oath when conditions in the Revolutionary forces were far from satisfactory. Yet, it is interesting to note that Moll had committed himself to the cause of freedom even before he took the oath. John Moll I was a member, Eighth Class, of the Third Company of the First Battalion of Northampton County Militia on June 18, 1777. "The militia was divided into eight classes. When a class was called out, many belonging to it, could not or would not go. The deficiency was made up by the employment of substitutes, either taken from the other classes, or from those not subject by law to the performance of military duty."[17] Moll was never called to active duty because his services were utilized in the state gun factory in Allentown.

In 1777 when food supplies were dwindling, ill-clothed and poorly-armed and trained soldiers retreated in the face of powerful British and Hessians. "As the British forces pressed on, Washington, fearing for the safety of the stores in Philadelphia and Trenton, ordered the Commissary and Quartermaster departments to cooperate in moving them to places of safety."[18] Thus a cartridge factory was relocated in Bethlehem, but had to be moved to Allentown because of unstable conditions. At the same time, as a result of Washington's order, a factory was established in Allentown for repairing arms and bayonets and the manufacturing of saddles. Captain Stiles was in charge of the military supplies while John Tyler and Ebenezer Cowell were armorers in the employ of the state who ran the factory. Cowell arrived in Allentown in 1777 and built the factory with timber from an old sawmill that belonged to David Deshler. Time, as in all wars, was a great factor for the arms had to be repaired as expeditiously as possible. It wasn't long before some sixteen armorers, of whom John Moll I was one, were actively engaged in repair work. Wood, procured locally, provided the necessary charcoal for forging operations as well as replacing the battered stocks of battle-worn rifles. Locally procured hides were transformed into saddles by craftsmen, while the water power of the Little Lehigh provided the necessary water power to turn grindstones which whetted colonial bayonets. They worked long and hard for small compensation and meager rations. However, the accomplishments were quite great. From October 15, 1777 to December 4, 1777 the factory received the following for repair: 7 pistols, 810 muskets, 847 bayonets, 360 scabbards, 36 rifles, 5 carbines, and 25 gunbarrels. In the period between October 15, 1777 and June 1779, the following repaired arms were shipped out from the Allentown factory: 7 pistols, 2 blunderbusses, 2961 muskets and barrels, 2522 bayonets, 685 scabbards, 83 rifles, and 5 carbines.[19]

On one occasion Moll came close to insubordination in protesting against conditions at the factory. Rations were extremely short and the workmen were threatening to stop work if they were reduced any further. It was on this occasion that John Wetzell, a Lieutenant of the county of Northampton, decided to notify his superiors on the Executive Council sitting at Lancaster of the unrest that existed.

My duty demands that I should give news to you of a new order received yesterday, viz, in relation to shortness of rations issued to military workers and saddlers, the same having created such great unrest among the workmen that they concluded to give up work. A conversation with David Deshler and Fred Hagener made them more content. The sub-lieutenants have received many arms to be repaired, and received yesterday four hundred muskets, and more are expected daily. The quartermaster writes that he wants a large quantity of repaired guns, because he is expecting new militia every day, as well as militia of this county, which is to be fully equipped. We have decided to allow former rations until we receive further instructions. Our department is now in good order, and is increased every day, so that I entertain the hope to obtain the necessary workmen to finish our labor.

P.S.—The rations which at present are issued are 1½ pounds of beef, 1½ pounds of bread, also flour and vegebatles, ½ pint of rum or whiskey, wood, soap, and candles.[20]

Nothing else is revealed concerning the incident.

Further evidence of the vast scope of the activities at the Allentown State Gun Factory are revealed in the following letters.

Allentown, May 9, 1778. Sir: In answer to your Favour of the 28th ult. I have to inform you that since the return of Arms I made on the 21st Jan. last, I have delivered Col. Fredk. Hagner two hundred and seventy two stand of arms in repair, and have now on hand three hundred and fifty stand complete, except half the number of bayonets are yet to be ground, but expect to have them all ground by 20th inst. The above 250 stand of Arms are all I have upon hand worth repairing, except a few that want new stocks, some of which I expect will be done before that time. I am, Sir, Mr. Most Obednt. Humble Servt., Ebenezer Cowell. (This was addressed to Thomas Wharton, Jr.)[2 1]

Two days later Frederick Hagener wrote the following to Thomas Wharton, Jr.:

May it please your Excellency; According to your Excellency and Council's last Request dated the 28th April, I have diligently examined and inquired into, but have not been able until this day to give a true and exact Account of what Arms, etc., are now in my possession and how many shall and can be properly repaired by the 20th of this month, which is as follows: In my possession in store, 800 Muskets & Bayonets, with Scabbards, 550 Bayonet Belts, 750 Cartouch Boxes, 45 Shot Punches and 118 Powder Horns...[2 2]

Hagener goes on to mention that the making of his quotas is dependent upon the efficiency of Tyler and Cowell. He states further that he will not leave a stone unturned to serve his country.

Thus, we can see that John Moll I definitely was aiding the country directly in repairing military equipment needed by the Revolutionary Army as well as being a member of the Northampton County Militia.

There is but one personal incident that is recorded regarding John Moll during the War and it can't be verified at the present moment. Charles Roberts stated that Moll had many beehives in his backyard, and that on one occasion he caught a Hessian prisoner stealing his honey.[2 3] Although it is true that Moll had quite an apiary and that the policy with the prisoners was one of leniency as far as confinement was concerned, Roberts doesn't reveal his source of the material. It sounds too much like a family yarn, its happening is not too remote. Needless to say the account neither states what happened to the prisoner nor the honey.

Evidently John Moll I had a hard time raising his family. True, supplies became more abundant, but prices soared so that the phrase "not worth a continental" became commonplace. "By 1780 business was prostrate, the closest economy required, and a still further disheartening complication arose from the depreciation of the public money."[24] The inflation that hit the Colonies was terrific. In Allentown, in 1781, sugar sold at twelve dollars a pound; coffee, two dollars; a silk handkerchief, one hundred twenty dollars; a spelling book, twenty dollars; a scythe, one hundred thirty dollars; tea, seventy-five dollars a pound; cambric, twenty-five dollars a yard; a skein of thread, four dollars; and a paper of pins, two dollars.[25]

In spite of lean years directly following the war, Moll, in later years, evidently prospered in his trade for in addition to a vast store of tools and personal property, he left quite a bit of real property in South Whitehall and Heidelberg Townships in addition to the property which he owned in Allentown.[26] John Moll I died in 1794 intestate. The contents of the inventory of his property reveals some of the following articles:

61 Beehives	2 Screw Plates and Pins
30 Hour Clock and Case	1 Bench Vize
Silver Watch	1 Bench Vize
40 Empty Beehives	1 Hand Vize
100 Riffle Stocks	32 Different Chisels & gouges
18 Riffle Locks	8 Moule Augers
1 New Riffle	5 different Planes
1 Riffle Barrel	13 Cut files
1 Smooth Riffle	3 Hammers

1 Cut Riffle	2 Pincers and 1 Plyer
1 Riffel Barrel & Stock	1 Polish Steel Plyer
1 New Riffle	1 Braech Pin Iron
1 Smith Bellows	1 Brace and Bitts
1 Anvil	2 Saws
1 Anvil	2 Dressing Knives
1 Large Smith Hammer	1 Grindstone
7 Smiths Hammers	1 Arithmetic
3 Smith Tonges	1 Spelling Book & Pr. book
2 Nail Plates	Song book and Psalter
1 Pig Iron	1 Scale and weights
Sundry Iron	5 tt Sheet Brass
2 Setts Riffle	5 tt Old Brass
Sundry Old Iron	Also 1 Riffle which war
Household Goods	forgot in the Inventory
3 Iron Augers	Riffle Augers
13 Riffle Augers	25 Files and Rasps

The spelling of the above items has been copied directly from the list. John Moll I was well-equipped to carry out his trade and gun collectors today have much to say of the fine workmanship displayed in the weapons he produced.

The final settlement of the estate amounted to three hundred ninety-four pounds, 15 shillings, and nine pence. The property was appraised on January 31, 1795. Lydia Moll received one-third of the estate as prescribed by Pennsylvania law.[28]

John Moll I was survived by his widow and two sons, John II and Peter.[29] There is no record of what happened to John J. Moll according to the source just mentioned. However, the wording of the legal document quoted below pertaining to Peter Moll, a minor son who survived, leads me to believe that John J. was still living. I believe that the key words in this document are "among other children". The document reads as follows:

At the Orphans Court held at Easton in and for the County of Northampton the tenth day of November in the year of our Lord one thousand seven hundred and ninety-five.[30] Before the Honorable Jacob Rush, Peter Rhoads, William Henry Esquire, judges of the said Court.

On the Petition of Peter Moll one of the Children of John Moll late of the town of Northampton, Gunsmith, deceased. Setting forth that the said John Moll sometime since died Intestate leaving among other Children the Petitioner who is now a minor above the age of fourteen years and is desirous of having a guardian. Praying that the Court would be pleased to permit him to appear and with the approbation of the Court make choice of a guardian to take care of his person and Estate. Whereupon the said Minor appeared in Court and did choose Abraham Rinker of the town of Northampton, Hatter, as and for his Guardian to take care of his person and Estate, who is approved by the Court and he the Said, Abraham Rinker, is so appointed accordingly.[31]

This information was gained by spotting a disbursement of twelve shillings and six pence on the final settlement account of John Moll I's estate.

Abraham Rinker was Peter Moll's uncle. This Peter Moll is not the man who came to Hellertown and set up a gunsmithing business. This Peter Moll is the uncle of the Peter Moll who came to Hellertown.

FOOTNOTES II

. 2. Matthews, Alfred and Hungerford, Austin N., **History of the Counties of Lehigh and Carbon in the Commonwealth of Pa.**, p. 123.

3. Roberts, Charles R., et al., op. cit., p. 390.

4. Roberts, Charles R., et al., op. cit., pp. 391-392.

5. Roberts, Charles R., "Early History of Allentown," **Annual Proceedings of the Lehigh County Historical Society**, Vol. XII, p. 83.

6. Henry, Matthew S., **A Manuscript History of Northampton County**, p. 39.

7. Roberts, Charles R., et al., op. cit., p. 1073.

8. Weiser, Charles W., "The Early Hotels of Allentown," **Annual Proceedings of the Lehigh County Historical Society**, Vol. VIII, p. 97.

9. **Northampton County Deed Book**, Vol. I E, p. 649.

10. Beckel, Clarence E., ed., **Zion Reformed Church—Allentown Records of Zion German Reformed Congregation Allentown, Pa. 1765-1861.**, p. 7.

11. **Ibid.**, p. 12.

12. **Ibid.**, p. 17.

13. Myers, Mrs. E. F. I., "The Northampton County Militia, 1776," **Northampton County Sketches**, p. 68.

14. Wilkinson, Norman B., "The Pennsylvania Rifle," **Historic Pennsylvania Leaflet No. 4**, p. 4.

15. Allentown Board of Trade, **Past, Present, and Future of the City of Allentown, Pa.**, p. 12.

16. Marx, Henry F. ed., **Oaths of Allegiance of Northampton County, Pennsylvania 1777-1784**, p. 35.

17. Roberts, Charles R., et al., op. cit., pp. 132-133.

18. Johnson, Victor L., **The Administration of the American Commissariat During the Revolutionary War**, p. 80.

19. Roberts, Charles, et al., op. cit., p. 140.

20. **Ibid.**, p. 141.

21. Weaver, Ethan Allen, **Copies of Revolutionary War Letters Relating to Northampton County, Pennsylvania.**

22. Roberts, Charles R., et al., op. cit., p. 141.

23. Roberts, Charles R., op. cit., p. 83.

24. Heller, William J., **History of Northampton County and the Grand Valley of the Lehigh**, Vol. I, p. 139.

25. Roberts, Charles R., et al., op. cit., p. 148.

26. See Appendix I.

27. **Northampton County Register of Wills**, File 1702.

28. **Ibid.**

29. Gardner, Robert E., **Arms Fabricators, Ancient and Modern**, pp. 60-61.

30. The punctuation in this document is mine which I inserted for the purpose of clarification.

31. Northampton County Orphans Court Docket, **Vol. VI, p. 11.**

III. THE LATER MOLLS AND THEIR ACTIVITIES

John Moll II carried on the business after the death of his father. The shop, as we have stated before, was located on what is now North Seventh Street. During the War of 1812, John II stayed at home producing weapons while his brother Peter answered the call of arms. Peter was one of the young men who on August 18, 1814 met in Center Square in full military uniform to be assigned to active duty. He was assigned to his uncle and guardian's company of Pennsylvania riflemen. Abraham Rinker's Company was a part of the 18th Section of Riflemen commanded by Colonel Thomas Humphrey. The unit was stationed at Camp Dumont. The muster roll of November 13, 1814 lists among others, Private Peter Moll.[32] Peter survived the war, came home, and died a rich man years later.

John Moll II joined with one of the oldest families of the county when he married Elizabeth Newhard, the eldest daughter of Laurence Newhard. From this union John III, Jacob, and Peter (who later set up business in Hellertown) were born. John III was born on November 13, 1796;[33] Peter was born October 13, 1799. One of his sponsors at baptism was his uncle, Peter Moll.[34]

Some historians would have us believe that John Moll III was in partnership with his brother Peter in Hellertown about 1810. This contention is rather absurd when we stop to realize that John III would have been only fourteen years and his brother Peter eleven. Yet one can enter the Philadelphia Museum of Art and read the label on a rifle "Kentucky Rifle, American, Pennsylvania, Hellertown, John Moll, c. 1810." The rifle referred to is engraved only with the name of "John Moll" behind the rear sight. John Moll III was never a partner of his brother Peter. Peter Moll's partner in Hellertown was David Moll. It is a fact that every rifle they made is plainly marked either with a name, a date, or a number. There is substantial evidence that John Moll III stayed in Allentown and worked with his father John II. For some unknown reason, probably sickness, John Moll II sold the business to his son John III on April 11, 1820.[35] The document of the sale recorded in the Lehigh County Court House. It reads as follows:

Know all men by these Presents that I John Moll of the Borough of Northampton in the County of Lehigh in the State of Pennsylvania Gunsmith for and in consideration of the Sum of one hundred and five dollars lawfull money of the United States to me in hand paid by my Son John Moll junior of the same place Gunsmith, at and before the ensealing and delivery of these Presents, the receipt whereof is hereby acknowledged have bargained, Sold and delivered and by these presents Do grant bargain Sell and deliver unto the Said John Moll Junior three Bench Kies, one grindstone, and boring Machine, two Screw Plates, Cut Bench and two Iron bars thereunto belonging twenty two Maple Blocks and thirty Stocks for Riffels, Fifteen Riffle Augers, One Bellows, Sixty Five Bushels of Coals, one polishing Machine, two Anvils, Seven Hammers, One Walnut Case of Drawers, One Bed and Bedstead, one Walnut Chest, one large Copper Kettle, two Hives of Bees and all the apparatus belonging to oure Foundery. To have and to hold all and Singular the Said Premises unto the Said John Moll, his Executers, Administrators, and Assigns.

Said in the prescence of John Horn and Philip Brong.[36]

It is interesting to note that some of the items that were sold to John Moll III were the same items that appeared in the inventory of his grandfather's estate.

John Moll III bought his father's business and managed to maintain an interest in the firm until his death in 1883. The business was a profitable one under his father's management for in 1814 the amount of tax paid by John Moll II places him twenty-fifth from the top of the list of one hundred fifty-two taxables. His tax, incidentally, amounted to one dollar and ninety-eight cents.[37]

I have mentioned previously that John Moll was never a partner in the Hellertown firm. However, the observing scholar might ask how I can explain the fact that a John Moll appeared at the preparatory services of communion at the Lower Saucon Reformed Church on April 13, 1827, April 10, 1830, and November 19, 1831.[38] If this is the same John Moll, I would explain his presence there as a part of a visit with his brother Peter in Hellertown. As far as can be determined John Moll III never maintained a residence in either Lower Saucon Township or Hellertown.

We can generalize at this point and state that a turning point came in the production of the rifle during John Moll's life. The flintlock had been replaced by the percussion type of lock. The early smiths had neither the time nor the inclination to deal in silver or brass ornaments. The Lancaster gunsmiths are an exception to this rule. The rifle was generally plain but superb workmanship made it beautiful.[39] On some occasions, when the customer demanded, the rule was broken and the gunsmith etched a design on the metal surfaces or carved the stock and inlaid the metal. "This custom was rarely followed by later makers. It was a practice of the Molls..."[40] Later models were more ornate, being loaded with silver, gold, and brass ornaments.

John Moll III lived a long full life. He was eighty-seven years old when he died. In addition to maintaining the family business of gunsmithing, he is listed as one of twenty-three Allentown merchants who, in 1838, offered foreign merchandise for sale.[41] He was successful in local politics on one occasion in 1844 when he was elected to the city council of Allentown at the time Peter Newhard was Burgess. The disastrous fire that swept the city of Allentown in 1848 causing 200,000 dollars worth of damage did not destroy his place of business.[42] Even though in later years when the business was taken over by his son William H. Moll, John III retained one-half interest. This interest was worth eighteen dollars as stated in the inventory of his estate. The firm then was known as J. and W. H. Moll.

John Moll III and Elizabeth Ueberroth were married in 1824. The following is an extract of the notice that appeared in the Friday issue of the *Freidens Bothe* on April 23, 1824: "Married On Monday last, by the Rev. Mr. Gobrecht, Mr. John Moll Jr., of this borough, to Miss Ueberroth, of Northampton Township, Lehigh County."[43] Numerous children were born. William H., successor to the business, was born on November 1, 1825;[44] Sarah was born September 23, 1827;[45] Mari Anne was born October 15, 1828;[46] Catherina was born March 27, 1830;[47] Tilghman Carl was born February 23, 1832;[48] and Josiah David was born March 30, 1838.[49] Josiah David was baptized on May 13, 1838 and had as his sponsors the heretofore elusive Nathan Moll and his wife Rosanna of Hellertown. The last child to be born was Franklin Enoch. His birth date was June 28, 1847.[50]

I cannot ascertain how many rifles they produced, but the census of Lehigh County in 1840 reports that four hundred sixty-five small arms were produced in that year.[51]

There were other gunsmiths in the county at that time; however, I cannot be sure whether or not the output of the Henry Factory at Boulton, Pa. is included in the total of four hundred sixty-five.

In 1860, at the outbreak of the Civil War, we find the first definite proof that John Moll III took his son, William H., into the business. James Moll, a relative, was employed at the factory and also lived there. William H., at that time, lived at 63 North Seventh Street.[52] The next list that we find is in the year 1873-74 when four Molls were engaged in the business.[53]

John Moll III died at 3:15 p.m. on Wednesday, August 24, 1883. He always carried the title of Gunsmith after his name and it even appears in his will.[54] He left all of his property to his wife Elizabeth and appointed his son, William H., as the administrator of his estate. This will was made in January 19, 1867. It seems that there was a defect in the will which failed to make provision for the payment of debts. Accordingly, upon his death, his widow sent the following letter to T. F. Keck, then Register of Wills in Lehigh County: "I hereby give notice that I refuse to take under the Will of my deceased husband, John Moll, but do elect to claim under the intestate laws of the Commonwealth of Pennsylvania. S/ ELIZABETH X MOLL."[55]
                      her mark

The inventory of the estate listed one-half interest in J. and W. H. Moll for Eighteen dollars and a one-half interest in a cemetery lot for fifteen dollars. The property on North Seventh Street was worth seven thousand five hundred dollars. This inventory was dated November 21, 1883.[56]

On January 31, 1884 an agreement between Elizabeth Moll and her children was made, which authorized William H. Moll to advertise the property and sell it either publicly or privately. William H. was to receive five percent of the sale price and the remainder was to be divided equally among the children after the death of the mother.[57]   Soon after this tansaction, the property was sold to Constantine F. Losek. Catherina Moll and her husband Nathan Deeker waived their share in favor of Daniel Geiser and his wife.[58]

Selling the property must have been a difficult decision to make as it had been in the family even before the Revolution. The sale of the property, in effect, completed the organized activities of the Moll gunsmiths of Allentown.

FOOTNOTES III

32. Roberts, Charles R., et al., **op. cit.**, p. 300.
33. Roberts, Charles R., **A History of the Newhard Family of Pennsylvania**, p. 4.
34. Beckel, Clarence E., **op. cit.**, p. 46.
35. **Lehigh County Deed Book, Miscellaneous Docket**, Vol. I, p. 144.
36. **Ibid.**
37. Roberts, Charles R., et al., **op. cit.**, p. 423.
38. Beckel, Clarence E., **Records of Christ Reformed Congregation Lower Saucon Township, Northampton County, Penna., 1756-1845**, pp. 123-124, 119.
39. See Appendix II.
40. Dillon, John G. W., **The Kentucky Rifle**, p. 36.
41. Matthews, Alfred and Hungerford, Austin N., **op. cit.**, p. 141.
42. Roberts, Charles R., et al., **op. cit.**, p. 433.
43. Marx, Henry F., **Marriages and Deaths—Northampton County 1799-1851**, p. 1447.
44. Beckel, Clarence E., **Zion Records, op. cit.**, p. 105.
45. **Ibid.**, p. 108.
46. **Ibid.** p. 111.
47. **Ibid.** p. 114.
48. **Ibid.** p. 116.
49. **Ibid.** p. 129.
50. **Ibid.** p. 141.
51. Roberts, Charles R., et al., **op. cit.**, p. 386.
52. Anonymous, **Boyd Business directory**, p. 87.
53. **Horlacher and Weiser's Directory of Allentown and Lehigh County**, W. J. Hexworth, comp., p. 84.
54. **Lehigh County Register of Wills**, File 6084.
55. **Ibid.**
56. **Ibid.**
57. **Lehigh County Deed Book, Miscellaneous Docket**, Vol. XVII, p. 361.
58. **Ibid.**, p. 482.

IV. THE HELLERTOWN MOLLS

Peter Moll of Hellertown, as we have said before, was the son of John Moll II and the brother of John Moll III. It is possible that Peter Moll appeared in Hellertown as early as 1820 when his brother bought the business from their father. Hellertown in 1820 contained thirteen houses, eighteen families, three taverns, two stores, one grist mill, and seventy-three inhabitants.[59] The first record that we have of Peter's residence in Hellertown is a rifle dated May 26, 1826, #40.[60]

In spite of the fact that Peter Moll and his partner, David Moll, made many fine rifles, they are most noted for their pistols which were of the secondary martial type.[61] A secondary martial pistol is one which can be made in several ways, namely, by an official contractor who made strictly federal weapons, by private contractors who were not official contractors to the United States, but to a particular state, by private enterprise for sales to individuals, or by manufacturing on a private contract with owners of vessels.[62] A search of United States Ordnance contracts leads me to believe that the Molls of Hellertown were not official contractors, but were contractors to the State, and also sold weapons to individuals. This point can be proved when one examines the pistols. One can distinguish at a glance the difference between the Moll contract pistol and the one made for sale to private individuals. The contract piece is a more rugged weapon and usually has a rifled barrel. These pistols were produced on a semi-mass production basis.

Assuming that guns made by Peter Moll were numbered consecutively, I have determined that he spent an average of two weeks to produce a rifle. Gun #40 dated May 26, 1826 and gun #51 dated November 2, 1826 are the basis for my calculation.

Peter Moll married Mary Shafer in the 1830's. Unfortunately the exact date is not known. An article appearing in the *Allentown Morning Call* dated December 5, 1929 which marked the one-hundredth anniversary of the gunshop in Hellertown, read as follows: "Peter Moll erected the shop,[63] now the Ruch Store, and moved into the place on April 12, 1831. He then married Mary Shafer and erected a dwelling, moving into it on July 26, 1831."[64] The land on which he built his home was owned by John Younghen who sold it to Christian Shafer on May 31, 1822. On December 5, 1829 the property was transferred from Christian Shafer to Peter Moll upon payment of one hundred fifteen dollars. The deed was not recorded until the 19th of March 1837.[65]

A partnership had been formed with David Moll, a relative of Peter's. David's true relationship to Peter can't be determined, but it is safe to assume that he was either a cousin or a nephew. At any rate, an article appearing in the *Frieden's Bothe*, Thrusday, December 10, 1835 read as follows: "Married On Sunday last by Rev. Mr. Jaeger, David Moll to Elizabeth Weber, both of Hellertown."[66] David Moll was born April 22, 1807 and it is assumed that he learned his trade from family craftsmen in Allentown.

The reader should take particular note of the age of these men at the time of the War of 1812. Peter was thirteen years old and David was five. Van Rensselear and other gun experts would have us believe that this partnership was busily turning out secondary martial pistols for the troops in the War of 1812. In fact Van Rensselear says in describing one of the pistols that "the silver name plate on the comb had an engraved "S" in Script on it signifying 'Sawken Light Horse Cavalry' as the author understands a troop was equipped with these pistols."[6][7] A similar pistol is owned by Lt. Col. B. R. Lewis, Ordnance Department, USA. In a letter to me he states that his pistol has the initials "AJ" stamped upon the escutcheon. There is no doubt in my mind that the majority of pistols produced had some type of initials engraved upon them. The point may seem trivial in some respects but it is a glaring error when one realizes, upon investigation, that certain individuals are guilty of romanticizing history. If the error was an honest one, it is time that it was corrected; if the statement was made to enrich local history and the prestige of the gunsmiths, it was dishonest.

"A search of the records of the War Department in the National Archives has not revealed information concerning the awarding of government contracts to the Moll family during the Revolutionary War, the War of 1812, or the Civil War."[6][8] A search of the patent records reveals that none have ever been granted to any member of the Moll family. This is no reflection on the quality or quantity of their workmanship. The greatest number of pistols that are in existence today from this period are signed "Peter and David Moll Hellerstown". This fact can be accounted for due to a contract that was awarded to them for 1500 pistols.[6][9] This contract has not been found, but in all probability, it was a local one. There is a good possibility that the contract might have been with the firm of Wolf and Bishop.

The Molls specialized in the brass-barreled pistols. The sporting type had a smooth bore, while the martial type had rifling. The stocks were made from plain maple rather than the more highly-desired curly maple. However, the Molls artificially grained the plain maple to make it appear like curly maple. This was done by wrapping a tarred cloth tightly around the stock, setting it on fire, and then burning it off. When the final finish of the stock was completed, dark traces of the burned strips gave it the appearance of curly maple. The Leamans of Lancaster also used this practice.[70] Dillon states that the pistols were a by-product of the rifles in that people thought it might be a good idea to have an extra shot on hand while reloading the rifle. More than likely the advent of cavalry had a lot to do with the popularity of the pistol.

The following is a description of a Moll pistol to give the reader an idea of the type of workmanship that was performed:

> Weight 1 lb., 9 oz., Octagon brass barrel 7 5/8 inches long marked in script, "Peter and David Moll Hellerstown", 13¼ inches overall, smooth bore cal. 46, full stock with painted reddish brown stock characteristic of Moll, heavy cast brass trigger guard, slight etching, butt cap extending toward stang, also etched cap, barrel pin fastened, 8 point silver barrel pin escutcheons. Imported lock 4¼ inches long and engraved, "S. Moore warranted," originally flintlock and altered to percussion, brass escutcheons for lock plate screws. This is the sporting type of pistol, barrel being highly polished, light in weight and slender.[71]

There is one illustration of a Moll pistol in the frontispiece. However, illustrations of several rifles are included.[72]

The Hellertown Molls were kept quite busy with making new rifles and pistols and repairing and converting older flintlocks to percussion type pieces. About eighty per cent of all flintlocks were converted to percussion types during the years 1835-55 at a cost of two to three dollars.[73] The Molls were also in the hardware business. They bought numerous tracts of land in Hellertown; one notable piece was purchased from Charles Wagner and wife. It was a ten acre piece located and bounded by the lands of John Woodring, I. Ott, and Jacob Rentzheimer.[74]

26

A typical rifle made by the Molls is still in firing condition today. It is dated January 30, 1833. A group pattern of shots fired, as well as the rifle itself, is illustrated in the volume cited below.[75] In addition to the rifles illustrated in the appendices, I had the pleasure of viewing four rifles made by Peter and Peter and David Moll of Hellertown, Pa. The rifles are numbered #51, #88, #142, and #122. They are in the hands of a private collector.

The partnership of Peter and David was dissolved with the death of David on August 31, 1853.[76] John Weaver was appointed guardian of David's minor children and he released Peter of his obligations when he received one hundred fifteen dollars from the sale of some of the personal effects of David.[77] Of this amount some sixty dollars was realized from the sale of his tools. The business, at the time of David's death, had $1712.86½ in outstanding credits. An inventory of the business revealed a well-stocked store with various and sundry hardware items such as:

Thumb latches; morter, turning, firmer and socket chisels curry combs; shoe, table, carving, and butcher knives; whetstones; bolts; planes; spur auger bits; brass wire; lead pencils; cork screws; spring balances; shoe and leather punches; garden hoes; chains; razor strops; glass, paper, and squares; braces; sheel shears; files; rasps; locks; frying pans; spectacles; saws; shoe nails; iron and brass candle stick holders; snuffers; sewing sets; shovels; axes; paint; and carpet bags.

600 Segars—$1.20, empty powder casks—.80, shot bags, percussion caps, etc.—$45.26, pistols—$7.78, shotguns—$67.25, shot and powder—$13.92, rifles and shotguns—$75.00, sheet brass—$45.67, 1 lot of rifles—$176.50½, ½ pound of powder—$.42, lot of rifle stocks—$28.20, coal and charcoal—$1.00[78]

The inventory taken on April 21, 22, and 23, 1856 by John and Samuel Weber totaled $2706.81¾. The final settlement of the partnership is listed elsewhere.[79]

After the death of David the business fell into the hands of William and Edwin Moll, sons of Peter. Nathan Moll, who occasionally receives mention in gun catalogues, was also connected with the business. I cannot determine to what degree. After the death of William Moll, the firm became known as Edwin and David Moll. By this time they dealt only in dry goods and groceries.

A discovery of the records of George Lee, Gunsmith, a one-time apprentice of Peter Moll, reveals some information about Nathan Moll. Incidentally, George Lee was also the son-in-law of Peter Moll by virtue of his marriage to Elizabeth Moll, Peter's daughter.

After he completed his apprenticeship and before he entered the Civil War, George Lee was located in Iron Hill. He made gunstocks for the firm of W. and E. Moll. He worked for Nathan Moll on numerous occasions including May 30, 1859, April 2, 1860, May 24, 1861, January 2-18, 1861, February 4-20, 1861, and all of April 1861. In July of 1861 he purchased the following articles from Nathan Moll: 4 lbs. of powder, 3 boxes of caps, and 6 flints. On September 11, 1861, he again purchased supplies from Nathan Moll: 12½ lb. of no. 3 shot, 12½ lb. of 5 shot, 4 sites, 1 bullet mould, 5 boxes of caps, 2 Sinter pistol cocks, and 8 lb. of powder. He even lent money to Nathan Moll ad the following is the promissory note inscribed in the record book: "July 31, 1861, One year After Date I promise to pay to George Lee on order Sum of Sixty nine Dollars without Defalcation for value received with interest. S/ Nathan Moll"[30]

There is also a reference in the record book that George Lee did plating work for the Molls. He preferred to use walnut for his stocks.

After the Molls went into the dry goods business and after Nathan Moll had left for the West, John J. Moll, a grandson of Peter's, repaired guns as a sideline until the early 1900's in Hellertown. Peter Moll died at 8:00 p.m. on June 8, 1879.[81] He must have been ill for a long time for the estate amounted to only $216.98. His doctor, W. F. Detweiler, presented a bill to the estate amounting to $98.00, a considerable sum in those days.

FOOTNOTES IV

59. Heller, William J., **op. cit.**, Vol. II, p. 518.

60. Dillon, John G. W., **op. cit.**, Plate 121, n. p.

61. Chapel, Charles E., **Gun Collectors Handbook of Value**, Chapter IV.

62. **Ibid.**

63. See Appendix III.

64. **Allentown Morning Call**, December 5, 1929.

65. **Northampton County Deed Book**, Vol. V F, pp. 198-199.

66. Marx, Henry F., **Marriages and Deaths, op. cit.**, p. 1569.

67. Van Rensselear, S., **American Firearms, An Histology of American Gunsmiths; Arms Maufacturers, and Patentees**, p. 170.

68. **Heffner-Wood Letter**, April 30, 1953.

69. Dillon, John G. W., **op. cit.**, p. 126.

70. **Ibid.**, p. 28.

71. Dillon, John G. W., **op. cit.**, Plate 129.

72. See Appendix IV and V.

73. Dillon, John G. W., **op. cit.**, p. 121.

74. **Northampton County Deed Book**, Vol. VII D, p. 408.

75. Roberts, M. H., **The Muzzle Loading Cap Lock Rifle**, p. 277.

76. See Appendix VI.

77. **Northampton County Register of Wills**, File 6198.

78. **Ibid.**

79. See Appendix VII and VII A.

80. **Record of George Lee**, started May 14, 1859.

81. **Northampton County Register of Wills**, File 9958. See Appendix VIII.

V. CONCLUSION

This paper has attempted to record the activities of the Moll family in the manufacturing of small arms from the period 1747-1883. There is no doubt that much remains to be done with this basic work. If any success can be claimed for this paper it must be in the realm of clarifying the misconceptions that have existed over the years concerning the Moll family and the relationships of the various members of the family. I think that we have proved without a doubt that there was a definite relationship between the Hellertown and the Allentown Molls and that the family produced arms during a succession of critical times in the history of our country even though they didn't make the arms directly for the federal government. Perhaps one of the most satisfying accomplishments is the correcting of the fallacious notion that Peter and David Moll produced weapons for the War of 1812 and supplied the "Sawken Light Horse Cavalry" with them. The paper has stated that the Molls were generally noted for their fine craftmanship in the production of arms and this can be verified by the many gun collectors throughout the country today. I feel that we have presented an impartial account of the Molls' accomplishments. If the paper is open to criticism because of the objectivity and the lack of glorification of the family and their accomplishments, then let it be criticized.

What the total effect of the activities of the Moll gunsmiths was on the history of our country will never be fully appreciated or known since records have been destroyed or lost and the average person or historian does not have time to view the great picture in the light of relatively insignificant people doing the trade and work that they knew best. No matter what their contribution was to the sum total, one can be readily certain that they met the challenges of their day and performed to the best of their ability.

The clanging of the hammers of the early gunsmiths resounded over the country and the echo was the sharp crack of the flintlock which removed the menace of the Indians, won our freedom from the British, saved, our independence in 1812, preserved the Union, and settled the West The well-preserved rifle or pistol hanging neatly in a shining guncase of a museum is a monument to makers, like the Molls, for the gratitude that we owe them, as well as a symbol of the age that has passed. The ingenuity, resourcefulness, and perseverance that the early smiths displayed was responsible, to a large degree, for the rise and development of our country. The Molls can proudly take their position beside the Henrys, the Golchers, the Leamans, and hundreds of other Pennsylvania gunsmiths.

Appendix I: This is a view of North Seventh Street in Allentown, the site of the old Moll Gun Factory.

Appendix II: Flintlock rifle, marked on barrel on block letters "J. Moll". English lock, overall length 57¼ inches, barrel length 42 inches, curly maple, brass furniture, caliber .45, full octagon barrel. Courtesy of Paul Beret. and Robert A. Limons.

Appendix III: View of the site of the gun shop belonging to Peter and David Moll, Hellertown. All the property in view belonged to these men.

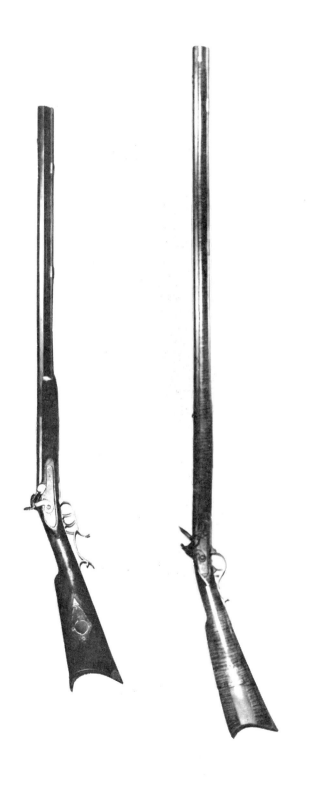

Appendix IV: Bottom view—Pennsylvania rifle "J. & Wm. H. Moll Allentown 2143" length 52 inches, barrel length 36 inches, caliber .40, inlays. Courtesy of Ed Minner and Robert Limons.

Top view—Converted flintlock, "P. & D. Moll, Hellertown", English lock, length 57 inches, octagon barrel length 42 inches, rope finish, no inlays. Courtesy of Paul Beret and Robert Limons.

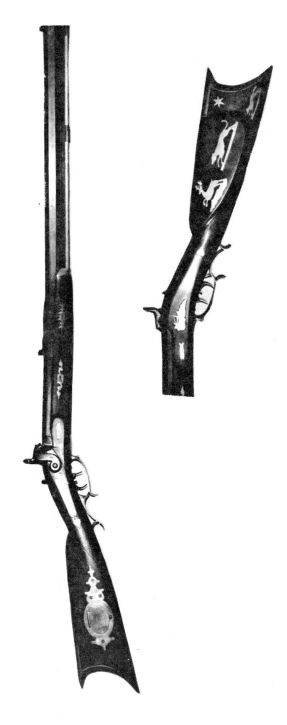

Appendix V: Top view—Percussion type rifle, "N. Moll" set in gold, length 46 inches, barrel length 30 inches, caliber .38, 13 silver and 4 ivory inlays, curly maple stock. Courtesy of Henry Nonnemaker and Robert Limons. Bottom view—Left side of stock of the same rifle.

Appendix VI: Graves of David Moll and Family. Located ½ mile south of Hellertown on Route 412. Name of cemetery New Jerusalem.

The account of Peter Moll (surviving partner of P & D Moll) and Administrator of David Moll Late of Lower Saucon Township in the County of Northampton and the State of Pennsylvania.

DR The said accountant charges himself with the following items to wit.

To Amt Rec'd for Rifles sold to Wolf & Bishop	$ 2024.03
To Cash Received of Goods sold in Store	5608.24¾
To Cash Received of Book accts collected	886.62
To Amount of Last Inventory	2706.81¾
To Amt of accountant family Expenses	726.08¼
To Amt received from John Woodring	150.00
	$12101.79¾
Balance as per contra on half belonging to the Estate of David Moll	$3666.13½
Amount due Estate of D. Moll decd.	$1833.06¾

Book accounts to the Amt of $269 are not collected if any the same will to the parties interested agree to make an amicable distribution of them.

Errors Excepted   Easton Oct. 21, 1859
Northampton ss
S/ Peter Moll
Peter Moll the accountant above named being duly sworn according to the Law Says the
S/ Thomas W. Lynn Regt.

APPENDIX VII   Debit Side of the Final Settlement
of the Peter and David Moll partnership

CR. The said accountant claims (?) credit for the following payment made for said Estate.

By Cash paid for hardward	$ 2371.00
By Cash paid for hardware	2024.03
By Cash paid Expenses on Rifles	707.47¼
By Cash paid Freight and other Expenses	315.50
By Cash paid as per Receipts on debts	1785.89
By Cash paid accountants account	529.92
By Cash paid as per Receipts	277.32
By Cash paid for Powder	398.18
By Cash paid Jacob Reed for Oil	26.35
Balance in hand of surviving partner	3666.13½
	$12101.79¾

Estate of D. Moll Cr.

Paid widow for family expenses	$ 425.85½
Paid debts as per Receipts	410.67
Paid debts and funeral expenses as per Receipts	315.52
Paid Mrs. Hillegass for sewing	1.16
Amt of goods accepted by Widow	258.43
Amt of goods accepted by Widow	14.60
Paid T. W. Lynn Register & O Fees	10.00
Val Hilburn Counsel fees	20.00
Debts of firm $20.73 4/10 one half is	10.36¾
Debts Isaias Bogenhorst $205.105 in above acct. ½	
Debts bal is	50.00
Debts Wm. Giersch 2.47½ one ½ of Bal	1.22
Amt of B 2/c loss $269 one ½ is	136.60
Accountants compensation	50.00
	$1702.42¼
Balance in hands of Accountant	130.64½
	1833.06¾

APPENDIX VII   Credit Side of the Final Settlement of the Peter and David Moll partnership

40

Appendix VIII: Graves of Peter and Mary Moll. Located ½ mile south of Hellertown on **Route 412**. Name of cemetery New Jerusalem.

VI. BIBLIOGRAPHY

1. Allentown Board of Trade, **Past, Present, and Future of the City of Allentown,** Allentown, Pa., Daily Chronicle and Newsprint Co., 1886.

2. **Allentown Morning Call,** December 5, 1929.

3. Beckel Clarence E., ed., **Records of Christ Reformed Congregation, Lower Saucon Township, Northampton County, Pennsylvania, 1756-1845,** Bethlehem, Pa., Under the direction of Harriet T. Root, Librarian, Bethlehem Public Library, 1939.

4. _____, **Zion Reformed Church—Allentown, Records of Zion Reformed Congregation, Allentown, Pa. 1765-1861,** Bethlehem, Pa., Under the direction of Harriet T. Root, Librarian, Bethlehem Public Library, 1939.

5. Chapel, Charles E., **Gun Collectors Handbook of Value,** New York, Coward—McCann, 1947.

6. Dillon, John G. W., **The Kentucky Rifle,** New York, Lidlum and Beebe, 3rd ed., 1946.

7. Gardner, Robert E., **Arms Fabricators, Ancient and Modern,** Columbus, Ohio, F. J. Heer Printing Co., 1934.

8. **Heffner—Wood Letter,** April 30, 1953.

9. Heller, William J., **History of Northampton County and the Grand Valley of the Lehigh,** Vol. I of III, Boston, Mass., American Historical Society, 1920.

10. Henry, Matthew S., **A Manuscript History of Northampton County,** 1851, (Hand-written copy)

11. Hexworth, William J., Compiler, **Horlacher and Weiser's Directory of Allentown and Lehigh County,** 1874.

12. Johnson, Victor L., **The Administration of the American Commissariat During the Revolutionary War,** Phila., Pa., 1941.

13. Lee, George, **Private Records,** started May 14, 1859.

14. **Lehigh County Deed Book, Miscellaneous Docket,** (Lehigh County Court House, Allentown, Pa.) Volumes I and XVII.

15. **Lehigh County Register of Wills,** (Lehigh County Court House, Allentown, Pa.), File 6084.

16. Marx, Henry F., Compiler, **Marriages and Deaths in Northampton County, 1799-1851,** (Newspaper Extracts), Vol. I of IV, Easton, Pa., Easton Public Library, 1929.

17. _____, **Oaths of Allegiance of Northampton County, Pennsylvania, 1777-84, also Oaths of Office from Orignal Lists of John Arndt, Recorder of Deeds 1777-1800,** Easton, Pa., Easton Public Library, 1932.

18. Matthews Alfred & Hungerford, Austin N., **History of the Counties of Lehigh and Carbon in the Commonwealth of Pennsylvania, Philadelphia, Pa.,** Everts and Richards, 1884.

19. Myers, Mrs. E. F. I., "The Northampton County Militia, 1776", **Northampton County Sketches, (a scrapbook of clippings).**

20. **Northampton County Deed Book,** (Northampton County Court House, Easton, Pa.), Volumes I E, V F, VII D.

21. **Northampton County Orphans Court Docket,** (Northampton County Court House, Easton, Pa.), Vol VI.

22. **Northampton County Register of Wills** (Northampton County Court House, Easton, Pa.), Files 1702, 6198, and 9958.

23. Roberts, Charles R., "Early History of Allentown", **Annual Proceedings of the Lehigh County Historical Society,** Allentown, Pa., Vol. XII, 1939.

24. _____, **A History of the Newhard Family of Pennsylvania,** Allentown, Pa., 1915.

25. Roberts, Charles R., et al., **History of Lehigh County, Pennsylvania,** Vol. I of III, Allentown, Pa., Lehigh Valley Publishing Co., 1914.

26. Roberts, M. H., **The Muzzle Loading Cap Lock Rifle,** Harrisburg, Pa., Military Service Publishing Co., 1947.

27. Van Rensselear, S., **American Firearms and Histology of American Gunsmith, Arms Manufacturers, and Patentees,** Watkin Glen, N.Y., Century House, 1947.

28. Weaver, Ethan Allen, **Copies of Revolutionary War Letters Relating to Northampton County, Pennsylvania,** Easton, Pa., Easton Public Library, 1930.

29. Weiser, Charles W., "The Early Hotels of Allentown", **Annual Proceedings of the Lehigh County Historical Society**, Allentown, Pa., Vol. VIII, 1924.

30. Wilkinson, Norman B., "The Pennsylvania Rifle", **Historic Pennsylvania Leaflet Number 4,** Harrisburg, Pa., Pennsylania Historical and Museum Commission, 1951.

Note: Due to the fact that the bibliography is small, I did not separate primary and secondary source materials.